THE EASY WAY TO
PROFOUND LIFE CHANGE

DESIGN
YOUR
FUTURE

ACTION BOOK

RAYYAN KARIM

"An inspirational coach"

- Adeel Mirza (Transformation Expert)

"Rayyan has a great understanding of business across different sectors... he gets to the heart of issues with ease"

- Mike Kessler (Founder of Tokenize)

"Passionate, dedicated, talented and a real critical thinker who wants action instead of words. Rayyan is rare talent... he's a thinker, doer and reflective practitioner in the world of constant change"

- Dr Paul Thomas
(Founder DNA Definitive & Founder High Street Fitness)

"Rayyan has rising star potential"

- Ade Shokoya (Digital Transformation Guru)

"Rayyan has the ability to move both the heart and mind with just his words. He's a go getter and inspires everyone around him to achieve results through an action based mindset"

- Farah Ismail (Inner Wellbeing & Fitness Coach)

Also by Rayyan:

Real Estate

— Luxury Real Estate in Dubai with Rayyan

Business Agility

— Start Up in 6 weeks or less

— Scale up in 3 months or less

— Leadership Excellence in 6 months or less

Personal Performance Coaching

— Design Your Future - The easy way to make profound life change - Action Book

— Design Your Future - Online Course

— 1-to-1 Coaching Support

Social Impact

— CBD Sanctuary Partnership with Tree-Nation helping to heal the planet

— Design Your Future - Youth Impact

Contents

Is This Book For You?

THIS BOOK

AIMS

TO UPLIFT YOUR SOUL

THROUGH

SIGNIFICANT ACTION

THAT YOU CAN

RINSE & REPEAT

IN YOUR TIME OF NEED

This book gets straight to the point

Yes, theory is important but what would you rather…

1) To have knowledge and not use it

2) To be using knowledge without knowing all the academic terms, theories and deep science behind it

I struggle to imagine why anyone would want to circle #1. Possibly they are hoping just to have something to talk about at the dinner table and are too scared to really "go" for making their best life experience happen.

In case you are wondering, personally, I would have circled number 2. This is because throughout my life I have always observed, questioned and reasoned with aspects of the world around us. Fortunately, I have had the pleasure of learning knowledge from some of the most experienced organisational and behaviour change experts that money can buy. Thanks to my own innate desire to constantly seek deep personal improvement and achievement on a bigger scale I have also been able to embed the theory into my own life.

As I got older, I realised that many of my early thoughts on what good business looks like or how to look at and navigate everyday life were aligned to academic theories and deep science. Naturally as I looked into the realm of academia around personal wellbeing, spirituality, and business there was a lot more also to learn - adding more metaphorical bows to my strings and more metaphorical feathers to my hat.

This action-book is definitely orientated more for the people who circled option #2 and less for those that circled option #1. Afterall, this is an action-book which hopes to inspire and guide you into the minimal set of activities and actions that will help you navigate change & change your life.

I wouldn't blame you if you circled neither, infact, the sensible and risk averse person would probably be left thinking that they want to have the knowledge and use it! If that's you, you're in the right place. That is exactly what this book is for.

Together we will make sure you appreciate big life changing concepts, approaches and methods in their simplest form so that you can implement them immediately, in the right order.

Simply, you will understand life changing concepts and approaches which I have personally applied to those that I coach personally, as well as businesses that I support to radically transform. This practical hands on action book is based on my real life experiences.

Easily you will appreciate these concepts and approaches at the highest level, then this action-book will guide you step by step in applying what you have learnt immediately!

Together, this book will help you make significant change happen in your life in the best possible way - with awareness, intention and dedicated passion.

This is what we are here to do.

We are here to simply learn from the life we lead so we can navigate life's lessons on our own terms. Yes sometimes life gives you lemons, and it's up to you and how you respond. Will you just make an ugly face and resist eating the lemon? Or, as the famous saying goes, will you turn that lemon into lemonade? My personally favoured approach is to eat the lemon with a smile on your face while you appreciate the vitamins are fast rushing through your body fortifying your energy.

That is to say, of course there are 'bad' things and some 'good' things that happen during our lives. How long they stay that way though is up to you. As you will see in this book, "bad" things often create the best things that have ever happened to us. Every 'bad' thing creates a beautiful moment of learning - although it does not feel like that at the time it happens.

We want to amplify your mind, your spirit and your body to the highest capability and heartfelt intention.

CHANGE

IS

UNCOMFORTABLE

LIFE

ACTION

Who Is Rayyan Karim?

Rayyan has worked with top leadership teams of worldwide FTSE100 & NASDAQ corporations supporting them to design and implement scaled digital transformation.

Rayyan is also a social entrepreneur with a non-profit making youth program that leverages neuro-science, behaviour-science and dramatic technique to inspire, motivate and guide young people to define their most compelling future as well as how they can make it happen.

Rayyan is also Co-Founder of CBD Sanctuary, a community-orientated planet first holistic health CBD brand that is focused on creating credible natural alternatives to the traditional over the counter pharmaceutical industry.

Rayyan and his hand-picked team currently leverage Rayyan's deep experience in 5 ways:

1. High net worth individuals to re-invest their capital in Dubai's booming real estate market

2. Founders, Co-Founders and CEOs to start up new revenue streams in 6-weeks or less from concept to cash flow generation

3. Managing Directors, CEO's, COO's and Sales/Marketing departments to scale up faster with a bespoke 3-month dedicated support program

4. Leaders of Medium and Large enterprises to enhance their leadership skills with a custom-fitted approach to maximising impact whilst sharpening your skills

5. People experiencing turbulent moments of change, transformation, challenge and opportunity through his Book, online course, and 1:1 support

What sort of life experience does Rayyan leverage in this book?

- From a juvenile criminal record to "Fast track to executive leadership" scheme at a top UK Bank

- Rescued $2BN relationship for blue-chip tech firms in less than 3 days

- From trainee to leading teams of 150 people across 10 teams in less than 3years

- From permanent employee £28k to £100k p/y contractor in 4years

- From corporate banking to Social Entrepreneur

- From £2.80 p/h working in a fish shop to a 1st class University degree in Accounting & Finance

- From boisterous angry adolescent to part time meditation teacher

- From traditional British bank to future-focused digitally enabled Bank of the Future

11

- From slow technology start up to rapidly growing technology scale up

- From initial holistic health business concept to generating revenue in less than 6 weeks

- From micro-business earning £1k per month to earning £1.5k per week in less than 10 weeks

- From the initial concept to inspiring 400 young people in one day with 9 of the world's technology giants in less than 6 months with only £50k investment.

This book is all about designing and attaining the future you want to have instead of whatever life throws your way. This is way more than the law of attraction. This is a step by step guide on how you can effectively navigate change and leverage the moment to make your highest aspirations and deepest desires happen.

Free well-being support

Available Worldwide

- United Global Mental Health Support

  - (https://unitedgmh.org/support/)

- Insight Timer

  - (Download and gain full access by downloading the Mobile App via Play Store / Google Store)

- Headspace Free Trial

  - (Download and gain full access by downloading the Mobile App via Play Store / Google Store)

Available in the UK

- Samaritans. To talk about anything that is upsetting you, you can contact Samaritans 24 hours a day, 365 days a year. You can call 116 123 (free from any phone), email jo@samaritans.org or visit some branches in person. You can also call the Samaritans Welsh Language Line on 0808 164 0123 (7pm–11pm every day).

- SANEline. If you're experiencing a mental health problem or supporting someone else, you can call SANEline on 0300 304 7000 (4.30pm–10.30pm every day).

- National Suicide Prevention Helpline UK. Offers a supportive listening service to anyone with thoughts of suicide. You can call the National Suicide Prevention Helpline UK on 0800 689 5652 (open 24/7).

- Campaign Against Living Miserably (CALM). You can call the CALM on 0800 58 58 58 (5pm–midnight every day) if you are struggling and need to talk. Or if you prefer not to speak on the phone, you could try the CALM webchat service.

- Shout. If you would prefer not to talk but want some mental health support, you could text SHOUT to 85258. Shout offers a confidential 24/7 text service providing support if you are in crisis and need immediate help.

- The Mix. If you're under 25, you can call The Mix on 0808 808 4994(3pm–midnight every day), request support by email using this form on The Mix website or use their crisis text messenger service.

- Papyrus HOPELINEUK. If you're under 35 and struggling with suicidal feelings, or concerned about a young person who might be struggling, you can call Papyrus HOPELINEUK on 0800 068 4141 (weekdays 10am-10pm, weekends 2pm-10pm and bank holidays 2pm–

10pm), email pat@papyrus-uk.org or text 07786 209 697.

- Nightline. If you're a student, you can look on the Nightline website to see if your university or college offers a night-time listening service. Nightline phone operators are all students too.

- Switchboard. If you identify as gay, lesbian, bisexual or transgender, you can call Switchboard on 0300 330 0630 (10am – 10pm every day), email chris@switchboard.lgbt or use their webchat service. Phone operators all identify as LGBT+.

- C.A.L.L. If you live in Wales, you can call the Community Advice and Listening Line (C.A.L.L.) on 0800 132 737 (open 24/7) or you can text 'help' followed by a question to 81066.

- Helplines Partnership. For more options, visit the Helplines Partnership Website for a directory of UK helplines. Mind's Infoline can also help you find services that can support you. If you're outside the UK, the Befrienders Worldwide website has a tool to search by country for emotional support helplines around the world.

<u>Design Your Future</u>

<u>Introduction</u>

Ideas, strategies, lifelines, policies, privacies, piracies…

We are all out to sea and its us that creates the momentum that blows our sails across the sea,

Believe, feel, explore within your skin and swim within your own perception,

Shine your own light on all that is around with your own outlook.

Zoom out now, examine the system of choices you make every day…

What choices could you make to turbo charge your change, clear your lane and elevate your day to day feelings?

- – Are you considering a career change?
- – Are you considering a location change?
- – Are you considering a relationship dynamic change?
- – Are you considering a direct, lifestyle, health / fitness routine?
- – Are you considering a spiritual / religious experiment?

- Are you considering a new way of managing your wealth?

- Are you considering a few routes of "giving back"?

Whatever it may be, every small choice you make everyday creates your experience of life. This can be broken down by your mindset through each passing moment. This mindset gets wired into you through your self-talk which cultivates the approach you take whilst you conduct the wide variety of tasks / activities we call life.

Every small choice is interconnected to your whole being and creates a ripple effect of energy. Just like your thoughts and your voice can change your emotions, this will also affect your energetic state physically and spiritually. Those three states of energy, physical, emotional and spiritual are all completely interlinked. Every lesson you lead your life through, every opportunity you take, every moment of conflict you experience, every good deed you do, and heartfelt conversation you have develops your state of energy. The energetic states I am referring to are physical, emotional and spiritual.

Trying an experiment to improve your life experience helps you to evaluate the impact your new twist on life has on your energetic states. An unbiased experiment looks at these three states both as independent parts and also as a combination of parts. It's as important to appreciate each energetic state as itself, comparing the impact before the experiment and after.

17

It is equally as important to appreciate each energetic state as being totally interconnected with the other two states.

This will help you understand what is truly good for you in a deep and long lasting sense. You will find this will develop your own ability to create conditions of a peaceful mind and heart which are the keys to long lasting peace, happiness and contentment.

Experiments are best run over 6 weeks, with a replanning of the experiment after every 3 weeks. It's also wise to check in on a daily basis on how you can maintain your commitment the best you possibly can. Similarly, on a weekly basis, deeper reflection on how you can become more consistent is also a wise choice. Turning old habits into new ways is no walk in the park and it takes personal resolve, absolute focus, full gratitude and a whole lot of letting go!

This next part of the book, Design Your Future, is dedicated to the process of creating your next most heartfelt and mind calming life decision. After all, once you fill your own energetic cups, you can fill others' energetic cups without needing them to fill yours in return and without using any of the water in your own cup. This could be an effective route for you to find the deep connection and love you desire, without the pain caused by the necessity of attachment and reciprocity.

In summary, this is a breakdown of the steps I recommend you take to implement the life evolving ideas that are likely to come to you through the next chapters:

1. Get absolute clarity your desired outcome, the benefits it will bring your life and of the step by step experiment plan

2. Take daily action and reflect regularly on how you can improve on delivering the experiments plan of action

3. Every week make sure you reflect on the actions you are taking and their impact on your life experience

4. When you hit week 3 purposefully create a moment of self-reflection to review your experiments success so far. Find 1 or 2 small improvements to try out.

5. At the end, on 6 week, create a powerful moment of self-reflection and holistically evaluate the impact it has had on your life experience. Think of this like a before and after! At this point you then decide what you will keep and continue to live with.

6. Find another area of life you want to experiment with and repeat from step 1.

Step 1 - Raise Your Investment

Increase the level of attention you invest in the choices you make every day. Afterall, the ultimate death scroll remedy is pretty obvious to most of us:

- Appreciate that every small choice can have a massive impact on your current experience of life and subsequent future

- Learn how to diagnose how effectively you are currently making your choices

- Create an action plan for raising your personal investment in life

What you give life is what determines your quality of life. Yes, there are a ton of reasons, histories, explanations, twists and turns and upside downs along the journey of life. We know there will be some sharp left turns and many unexpected events, all of which combine to alter your state of being, including the subtle bits below the surface which you may not be conscious of. As soon as we look at this life with awareness and we approach situations with increasing consciousness, magic moments of peace become possible.

It begins with a moment of clarity that you will still be able to pinpoint years later, just like Part 1 of this book. Who knows, maybe you will write your own book like this one day too. If you do, be sure to message me and I will do everything I can to help you. My hope is that the pages of the rest of this book create your pinpoint awareness moment. These short, succinct and sharp chapters with the following activities are to call you to action. Afterall, this is an action book.

When you look at the choices you make every day, there are always reasons. These are like default settings sometimes we don't even have awareness of them. Other times we think we know and yet we discover later we were deceiving ourselves with a too narrow point of view. Occasionally we have long held beliefs that stay true for long periods of time and seemingly never change. Whether you know your reasons or not, they are calling you into action. Even better yet, you are capable of stimulating and inspiring this process of self-improvement which gives you subtle control over your overall state of wellbeing at all moments.

You'd be within your right mind to think "what on earth does this fella know about the science and art of personal change and prosperity?"

I first was exposed to this knowledge through my mothers health condition which means I have always learnt about applying your mind and nurturing your own mindset to think limitlessly. I was also properly educated and schooled through University, a highly coveted Graduate Scheme, and many years of working with high performing teams in blue-chip businesses during huge transformations which fundamentally challenged every employee's identity. This taught me the science of personal change, team collaboration, high performance, personal excellence, leadership development and what was meant by "the art & science of fulfilment". This hands-on learning experience was funded by one of the biggest UK banks' and only because they had a desire to develop a brand new 'Bank of the Future". They wanted to create the best culture the world could ever marvel at and they needed to recreate an organisation from the ground up. There was an influx of incredible knowledge that I was simultaneously applying to various programs, some software, some HR teams, some retail centres as well as various processes and practises inside the Bank (such as their Apprenticeship pipelines and talent scheme). In just 3 and a half years I was able to gain deep practical experience in the science and art of personal and organisation change. Quite simply, because its people that are the real secret ingredient of all business success, the two areas of personal and organisational change are very interlinked.

Very intensely I studied and applied: complex adaptive system change, personal / life coaching, human change psychology, NLP, leadership, self-organising teams, software development at scale, systems thinking, customer journey and value stream design, rapid prototyping, agile development, developing inspiring visions. Literally everything the new world of banking would need rolled up in one intense 3 and a half year experience which set me up for the rest of my career.

Through this time I worked with 5 different Executive teams in a variety of roles. To start with I was the servant-leader of 1 team of 10, then for a team of 30 across different time zones, then for a team of 70 people and also becoming an expert helping to guide the central transformation method team. My last role there was as a full time "agile transformation coach" helping to restore faith in banking by helping customers in financial difficulty gain a more powerful banking relationship that would truly support their all round life experience.

It was during my last role at the big UK bank that i began Tai Chi and very soon i decided to leave and join a fast growing, forward thinking, FinTech. Directly this decision was due to my own experiments with visualisations and meditation. This cemented to me realise just how deep human change is. It runs throughout human history, through our veins, its in our blood, in our stitching, even our distant ancestors are still connected to us and are still changing with us! This is a very deep level of contemplation that is also backed by modern science.

Many ancient people had the knowledge of personal and organisational change and they harnessed it in a variety of ways. Have you ever noticed that the essential tenets of all spiritual ways of life, be they religious or just principles for living, that they always centre around the same essential tenant? My own personal observation of religion, spirituality and science is that the intersection that binds them all together is the observable and evidence based fact that there is a fundamental life energy that connects all things together. Naturally there is a difference of opinion on what to call that life energy and how to best nurture our sense of it - which I believe is up to each of us to determine for ourselves.

Incredibly, this means human change is as natural as the air that you breathe and the DNA that is running through you right now has a long history of success with change. After all, the cells on your skin, face and body are changing within a millisecond basis very faintly so subtly but they are changing. Imagine eating a banana, what happens within 20/30 mins of you digesting it? It becomes you! Some of it you take directly into your system and later you will deposit the rest out! Incredible really but we can easily forget in this modern world that what we consume literally becomes us. That is why we need to be more purposeful and decisive about where we spend our time, the activities we choose, and the things we learn to say yes and no to.

The amazing thing about combining spirituality with a scientific approach is that you start to understand both logically and experientially what is happening for yourself based on your own rationale and senses. All of this begins with experimentation, self-designed experiments that aim to boost your overall sense of vitality and wellbeing.

In short, choose your consumptions carefully to boost your sense of energy, life, wellbeing and health and make sure you learn the power of suggestion. The part of your experience that is unaware of your conscious mind, often referred to as the unconscious or subconscious mind, still responds to the stimulus you feed it and this influences your conscious states, decisions making and emotional flows. This part of you can be suggested too with images, visions, pictures, words, poetry, films, nature, and our physical environment including the language we use when we talk out loud and in our own minds. Yes, we all talk to ourselves!

Simply by engaging in the right pen and paper activities with the intention of making decisions about how to improve your life is your path to beginning incredible life change. By combining the eastern experience with western definition of personal change you can gain a strong combined sense and understanding of personal fulfilment and success.

As a result of blending these two together, some of the exercises may feel more comfortable than others. This is a pleasant time to remind you that "growth" by definition is not "comfortable". Growth is beyond what you have right now, so it will mean venturing into the unknown in the very beginning. This means we have to get comfortable with the uncomfortable and enjoy that chaotic feeling of not knowing what could happen next - yet trusting yourself to respond in the most heartfelt, hopeful and supportive way.

Just try, just play, just explore.

Make a list of good and bad choices you are making right now:

Rayyan

Good:

Fruit Smoothies

Beach yoga

Morning meditation

Prayers

Mind my words

Location change

Bad:

Unhealthy Dinners

Smoking cigarettes

Still working and stimulating my mind at night time

Not taking enough days fully 'off' work

<u>You?</u>

Good

Bad:

My moment of first awareness was at a bail hearing on my 18th birthday. The bail hearing heard me defend myself. I won't comment further here and all I will say is that this was my first realisation of there being multiple 'faces' or layers co-existing at once. These "faces" are just different layers of perception that co-exist at the same time. We all think differently, and some of us think multiple ways at the same time. This means when a room of people are together there are many layers all coexisting. They say in coaching circles that there are 3 levels of listening. The Japanese talk of the 3 faces, these two are very related.

"Either you are a world class fraudster… or you are telling the truth"

This moment opened my eyes to the choices that a person could actually make. Instead of following my unconscious default behaviour which led me to a life of regular low level crime, I could actually use those talents in other ways. It was the word "world class" that opened my eyes. The people at the bail hearing thought that possibly i was of world class calibre. This was the first time I actually thought that if I could find a better way to use my natural attributes then I could become far more than a low level criminal. In fact, with words like "world class" being associated with my name, I realised that crime was something that I didn't have to do. Instead, i needed to chart my own path out of my area and into the 'big time'. First, i had to think about what 'big time' meant. My first inspiration was being a suited and booted city slicker with a posh english blond and blue eyed lady on my arm. I achieved this at age 26, which we have explored in Part 1.

You see, Young people in the UK just want access to some fun, some enjoyment, and a good time. Most of us don't have money for this so we start looking at alternative ways to make money which of course then leads you to buying and selling, stealing and selling, and reckless behaviour. If only we were taught how to make the most out of our youthful fearlessness and energy. Unfortunately we are not taught how to approach complex life situations, how to navigate the society we live in, and how to stay clean hearted.

For personal improvement you need to ruthlessly focus on what you can influence and what you can control in your life, everything else is irrelevant.

What areas of life can you control?

Rayyan: Health, Wealth, education, mindfulness, leisure

You:

What areas of life can you influence?

Rayyan: work, family, intimate relationship, friendships, community

You:

Step 2 - Learn your "self"

Gain an understanding of who you are, what's important to you and why:

— Illustrate an understanding of who you are

— Highlight your top 3 values

— Appreciate values change and alter our perception

— Learn the layers of mind that create your character

I've never liked that question, "who am i". It was always so hard for me to logically follow to a conclusion so I then tried to see what might happen if I simply closed my eyes and meditated on it. Instead of thinking on it, just use it as a drum beat to guide the wondering mind. It's like seeing a picture reel unload all possible ancestors and walks of life and energy types. Like a home cinema that when you focus the mind on this question your mind unfolds different suggestions from past moments of time.

Truth is, a much better question that is getting at the same thing is really "what are we" and "how are we". In fact, as they are all interlinked, the mind, body and spirit combine together to create the life experience we have. What we are is determined by us either with or without awareness. Another way to understand this is that we determine how we are, what we are and also who we are with every passing moment either consciously or unconsciously. Either way, knowingly or not, we are in the driving seat and all we need to do is make the right choices for the journey we are on.

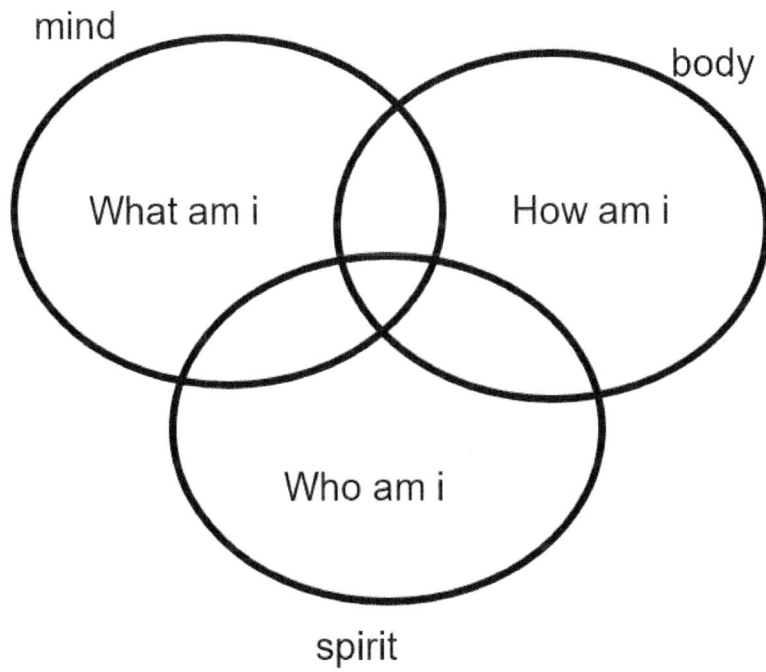

How we are is easiest to learn by checking into your body, how it feels, what emotions it sparks in the mind. Working the body can therefore help you transcend issues rooted in your mind. From my own personal research the Taoist, yogi's, sufi's and muslims all agree that when you combine the three dimensions of energy (physical, emotional and spiritual) consciously it brings your life experience closer to being in alignment with God / the source of creation / the universal life force / the "unified field" (as coined by modern science quantum theory). Supreme ultimate health and wellbeing should always be your ultimate aim, as this is the root of being able to support yourself, connect with the raw essence of life, and be a positive force in your family, social groups and wider community.

Check in with your body now, how does it feel? What aches and pains are you experiencing? Any tightness or soreness? Or are you able to stay fully relaxed yet energetically switched on and ready to flow peacefully through whatever life has in store for you?

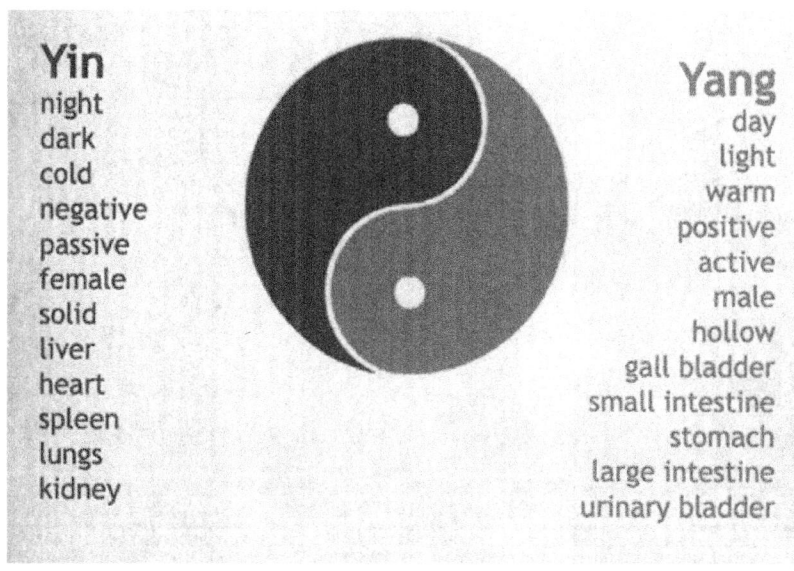

It could be argued that it is your first breath that sparks life as you know it. This means the unseen air is the real giver of life. Magic happens when this human instrument is sparked by the air that we all breathe, share and completely take for granted. This air is also seen in outer space and pervades all things -

even water and food are made as the same raw components as the material in the galaxy and beyond. This combination of air and the history (or memory) of your inherited energy makes you who you are right from the first gasping breath you ever took. In this way, the tangible and the intangible combine in perfect matrimony to create a very rare and unique life - YOU!

Some could refer to this process as the Yin & Yang dynamic, or as Tao, or as Allah / God.

Let's focus on your understanding of you right now, with this activity.

Draw this out and complete the questions:

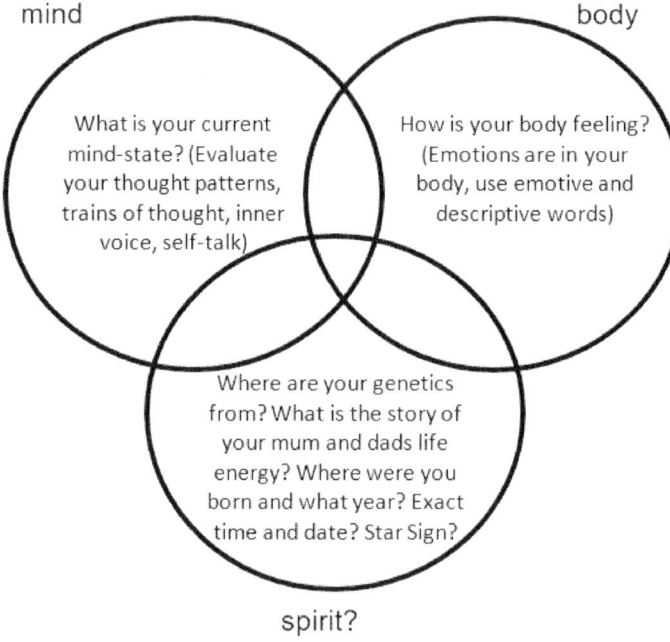

mind

body

What is your current mind-state? (Evaluate your thought patterns, trains of thought, inner voice, self-talk)

How is your body feeling? (Emotions are in your body, use emotive and descriptive words)

Where are your genetics from? What is the story of your mum and dads life energy? Where were you born and what year? Exact time and date? Star Sign?

spirit?

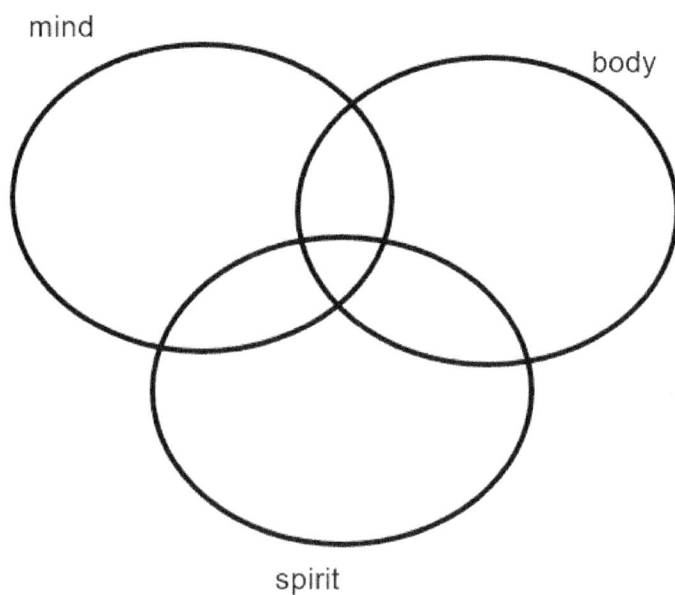

mind

body

spirit

For two years running I invested every monday evening in the park with my dad's best friend, Big Rick. Or as everyone outside his family would know him, Ricardo (learn more about Ricardo: www.TaiChiBalance.london). This man changed my life simply by spending time in a local park regularly experimenting with mindful movements with the ultimate aim of finding stillness in motion. To this day I am still discovering new elements and experience in the exact same 15 minute daily routine. The routine may be the same but your energy and surrounding context in every dimension has evolved (energetically, politically, economically, solar system, seasonality). It may seem subtle on a daily basis but over a period of days / weeks / months the subtle differences of the raw essence of nature and how they feel within your own experience are able to be sensed. It becomes like riding a bike through the park, it's the same bike, it requires the same motion from you but the park and the surrounding area of the park is different moment to moment every day.

Tai Chi was a must for me, with the doctors analysis being conclusive - at just 26 years old the bones in my neck were worn, my lower back too and my spine generally wonk causing pain, discomfort and increasingly impacting my day to day life. It wasn't a good picture for a 26 year old. However, in just 6 months the pain became manageable and after 18 months my body was painless, helping to soothe my cognitive and spiritual energy too. Four years on it has become an integral part of my life to be in sync with the natural ebb and flow of my inner environment - it brings me to peace and keeps me

35

grounded in what is really happening. As discussed in part 1, my main practice now to maintain my skeletal health is the 5 prayers per day.

At 26 I was living a pretty unhealthy lifestyle of fast food, beer, sugary food, tons of coffee and a bucket load of cannabis. Even though I was climbing fast through the world of big business transformation, my inner wellbeing was deteriorating fast. I had piled on more fat than I would have liked the mirror to allow me to see! Tai Chi was the catalyst that got me working for myself again. Simply by dedicating that first moment of every day to being invested in my own sense of personal well being transformed my entire life perception.

The question at the helm of what we are discussing is "what is the level of investment that we pay each of the choices we make every day?" How much of this is conscious / unconscious? Can we be sure that we are putting our energy into the right place for the life we truly want to lead?

Time for the next activity. How would you rank the following areas of life in terms of the amount of energy you focus on them?

Take some time now and rank them

(#1 being where our energy flows the most powerfully and #6 being where your energy flows the least powerfully):

Certainty

Uncertainty

Connection

Love

Growth

Contribution to society

When you consider the ultimate "you" that you would like to experience, do you see this future version of you behaving with the same ranking as the current you?

What would the future version of you look like?

Take some time now and rank the same areas of life but this time thinking of your future you:

_____

_____

_____

You see we have several layers that occur simultaneously at any given time. These layers are co-dependent yet are significant parts that we can at least gain a sense of by looking at them separately. You could see this as the onion of life, it starts with our Identity at its core, then our values, then our beliefs, then our behaviour and then our environment. This chain reaction combines to produce our experience of life and it can be influenced by us and others at any moment and in many different ways. When you break this chain reaction down, it becomes possible to consider ways of intervening to create the experience of life you really want. Start to evaluate how this chain reaction positively impacts your life, and assess what interventions you could make, so that its overall quality and effectiveness is well oiled for giving you what you really want. Use this tool to light your inner fire and reclaim your energy source so that you can be in the driving seat of how you experience this life.

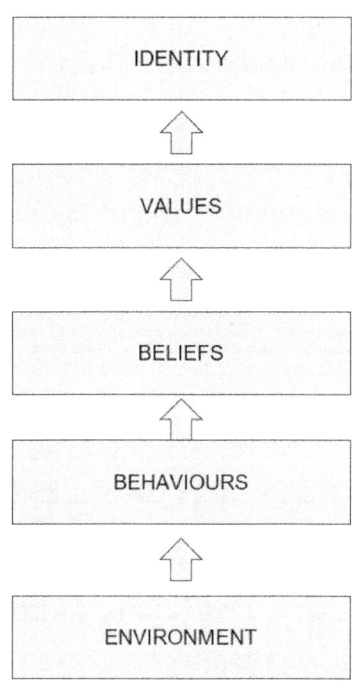

In my opinion this is the purpose of life, to be able to watch and understand life itself and enjoy fully everything you experienced for its ultimate good so the energy you started with leaves in a higher energy than it began. In a nutshell, it is my belief that we are here to become more at peace, with more good deeds than bad, and therefore enable our DNA to be recycled into the cosmos in an even more powerful state than it entered.

What level of the chain reaction described above did you last make a change in?

Did you intervene in your thinking at all?

Did you start a new exercise routine?

Did you start having detailed conversations about your parents lives?

Perhaps you went back recently to where it all started?

Take a moment to reflect right now:

What has changed for you most recently?

_____

_____

_____

Did it improve your overall sense of wellbeing? If so, how? If not, what else could you experiment with?

_____

_____

_____

LLOYDS
BANKING
GROUP

GRADUATE LEADERSHIP
& INTERN PROGRAMMES
APPLICATION

<u>Step 3 - Appreciate Your Self</u>

Gain deeper appreciation that people behave in the way they do, as a result of how they think of themselves and ultimately how they identify due to the chain reaction explained in the last chapter:

—   Diagnose self-talk, applying it to others and your self

—   Visualise, imagine and consider how life's experiences are different moment to moment because of our self-talk and self-identification

—   Become aware of the chain reaction of events that create our experience of life / ultimately ability to fulfil our destiny.

As well as the chain reaction of events that we explored in the last chapter there is also a profound sequence of energy that moves in stages and creates our experience of life:

Thoughts → Emotions → Actions → Behaviour → Habits → Destiny = Life Experience

Imagine the sequence of energy if these were your starting thoughts:

•   "This is a load of bollox…"

•   "I don't even like that though…"

- "init! That pisses me off…"

- "ah man you know deep down i'm still angry at _____"

Often our minds can replay unhelpful and restricting thoughts, or so it seems. Definitely there are events of the past that still run through our subconscious minds and connect the present experiences to some of those events through the shared memory bank of emotion that ties our subconscious and conscious experiences together. Emotionally they build one another and ultimately they layer on top of what was already there.

Occasionally we gain control of the chain reaction described above and truly live our best lives. Other moments we find that there are moments where we slip into bad habits that we ideally want to live without. It could be as simple as losing consistency with a routine, or drinking alcohol excessively or smoking or eating unhealthy foods etc. This makes us live at a lower frequency than in the moments that we are able to guide and directly influence our chain reaction of events for our most powerful frequency. Therefore, experiments are our way to having the emotional and energetic chemical soup that we cook up every day with our conscious and unconscious actions. The flavour of this chemical soup, could be called our life experience.

Whilst you undertake moments of interventions on this scale I've found it best to keep your curiosity objective and deeply empathetic. Really allow yourself to openly analyse the full spectrum and range of different avenues that are running at each stage of the chain reaction. You will have some obvious and some not so obvious chain reactions. Some will be tied together in a complex web of chain reactions, and others will be standalone.

The main thing is you know where you are now, and then what you want in your heart. You could see it like an objective self-assessment like a personal MOT:

Activity - Complete this for you now, in this moment

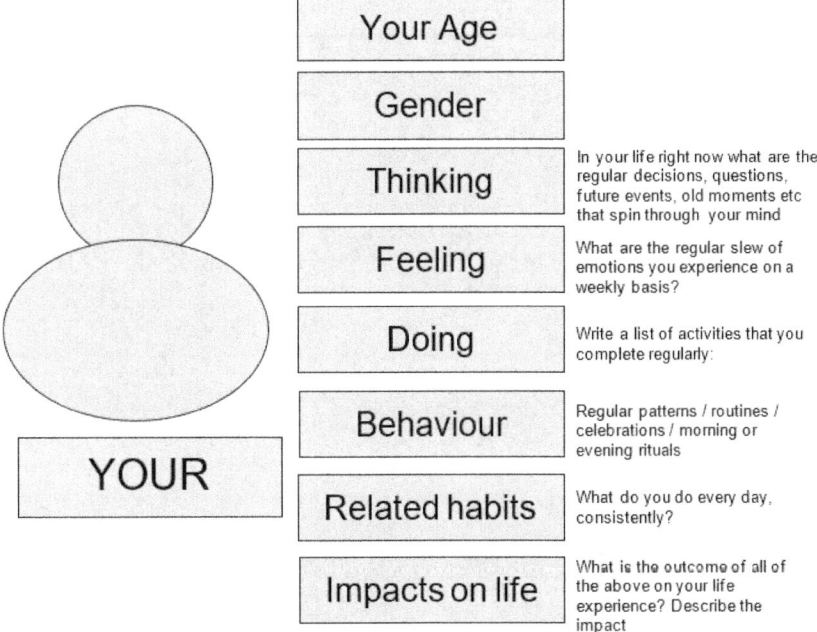

Your Age	
Gender	
Thinking	In your life right now what are the regular decisions, questions, future events, old moments etc that spin through your mind
Feeling	What are the regular slew of emotions you experience on a weekly basis?
Doing	Write a list of activities that you complete regularly:
Behaviour	Regular patterns / routines / celebrations / morning or evening rituals
Related habits	What do you do every day, consistently?
Impacts on life	What is the outcome of all of the above on your life experience? Describe the impact

YOUR

Notes:

Activity - Complete this for your most heartfelt future you

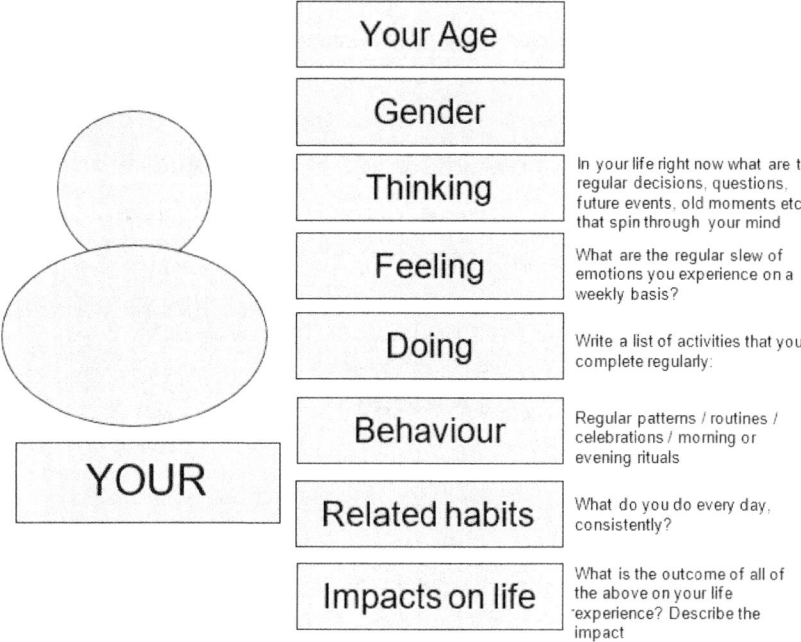

Your Age	
Gender	
Thinking	In your life right now what are the regular decisions, questions, future events, old moments etc that spin through your mind
Feeling	What are the regular slew of emotions you experience on a weekly basis?
Doing	Write a list of activities that you complete regularly:
Behaviour	Regular patterns / routines / celebrations / morning or evening rituals
Related habits	What do you do every day, consistently?
Impacts on life	What is the outcome of all of the above on your life experience? Describe the impact

YOUR

Notes:

Now that you have framed what you want, have spent the time imagining it, have written it down and openly explored its various aspects you will feel full of energy, hope and aspiration. By focusing on your most powerful future you are allowing your energy and natural intention to flow like a peaceful yet steadfast winding river.

The chain reaction, and the awareness of it, becomes your day to day practice. A great game to play when you have a cup of tea, or go for a walk, or you're in the bath, or meditating etc is to let your mind replay the events throughout the day with a lens of the profound sequence of energy explored in this chapter. See it in its various stages and explore how that energy has travelled throughout your recent life experience. You will benefit from going deep on each part of the sequence, one at a time, and then move onto the next. Once you can string together a few examples of the profound sequence of energy then you will be equipped to really go after your most empowering and heartfelt life experience. This tactic will help you learn how to check in with your subconscious (aka unconscious) and navigate towards what feels like it will give you the best zest for life.

What if you learn of an unhelpful thread?

Simply map it out:

Thoughts → Emotions → Actions → Behaviour → Habits → Destiny = Life Experience

And then challenge yourself…

- Thoughts: "what would be the empowering opposite thought?"

- Emotions: "How would that make you feel?"

- Actions: "What does that look like physically in your life?"

- Behaviour "How will you navigate life? What routines do you have? How would you describe your mindset?"

- Habits: "What will you do routinely? What practises or activities would be 'normal' for you?

- Life Experience: How would you rate your current vibrancy of life if this was happening? If full power was 10/10 what would you give this future state?

- If you need to create an action plan consider each of these questions in sequence to get to a resolution: How could you begin? What does an initial experiment look like? When will you learn if the experiment has had an impact? How can you guarantee that you take a moment to reflect and see if this has helped you? Now grab your phone and add yourself a calendar invite saying "Review chain reaction experiment" so you can gain your own understanding of this and not mine.

Later today allow yourself to day dream and consider the life of someone you know well, or at least someone you think you could apply the profound sequence of energy to. This is just a playful exercise so you can get more accustomed to playing with it. Notable people throughout history are a great place to start, sports people, inventors, people that have changed the world, musicians etc. The point is to zoom back to their top moments and see if you can apply the chain reaction to them in that moment. This will give you a deep level of empathy and understanding for what supreme life experience feels like.

Step 4 - Design Your Future

- Paint a vision of your self in the future including what you see, hear, feel.

- Design an avatar and really get into your future shoes

I've experienced that when your deepest desires and your unadultered, unconditioned sense of self combine there is heightened power in your ability to be steadfast while you navigate your own way to your improved life experience.

We must first learn what our conditioning is, how it shapes our outward / external personality and how it is different from that unchanged element within you that is always there yet not changing from its course, just deepening in its calling. This calling is your inner longing to be at your best. Once we unlearn our condition we gain a deep sense of perspective on how the interactions of society, family, friends, news channels, the workplace, your social media streams and (just about any and all information source) influence our outward expressions. The Japanese believe in 3 faces: the one strangers see, the one your closest people see, and the one that it's only possible for you to see (because it happens within your own experience and doesn't require expression for you to understand it). After all, who, other than you, can know what is truly in your heart when you are navigating through life's complexities.

Time to face the realities, face on, and to brutally cut the shit. Time to look at yourself, your innermost face, and be objective, honest and direct about your self and what you want for your experience of life.

Create the space for clarity to emerge.

When we think of our future we can easily get distracted by a vision of wealth, of greater social status, of material gain, of an enhanced career, beautiful holiday moments, expensive watches, luxury cars, restaurants and many different possible external events. To me, this sounds a lot like the narrative of success that is great for greasing the wheels of the current global economic system and the hierarchy of status that also replicates throughout many societies. However, that doesn't mean that it is the right, or only way of seeing success. Yes, we do live in a society that influences us to behave and think in this way and yes it is useful to know where these suggestions come from so that you can take back control of your life experience. These outside agents enter our life without our choosing, at random moments in time, simply due to the dynamic of the technological and information rich society we find ourselves in. This way, you can begin to choose what you consume, and you can choose your influences by becoming aware and making different choices.

At all times it is our deepest heartfelt desires that should guide us, otherwise we will end up unsatisfied and frustrated continually. This means we need to soul-search and be able to know the difference between the presenting opportunity (what we think the future looks like) and what's really going on (the real, deeper, inner sense of wellbeing that you are really searching for).

What do you want to experience in the future? How about exactly 10 years from this day, how do you want to feel? What do you want to be doing? What do you have in your life? How will you define and rank the key aspects of life? Who will be around you?

Example & Then Your Turn

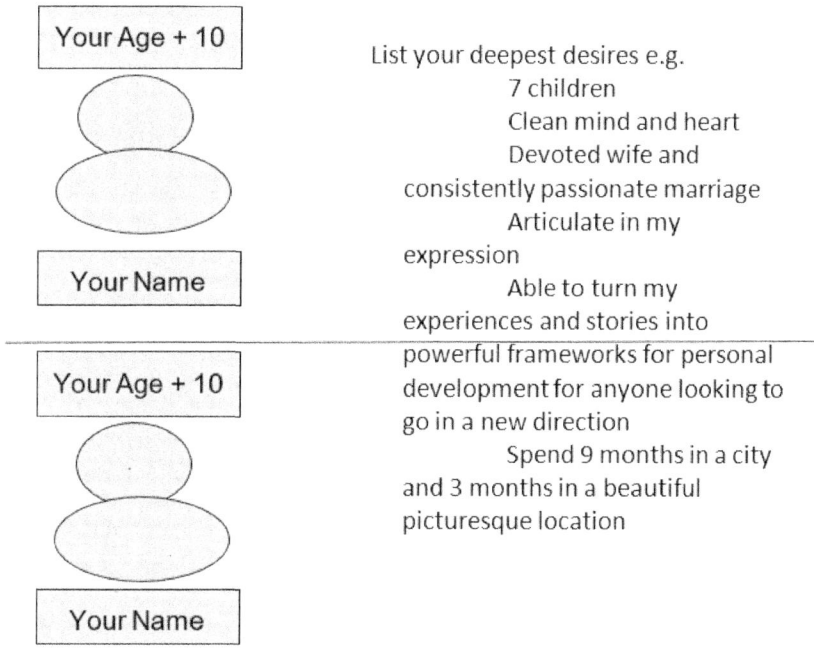

List your deepest desires e.g.
7 children
Clean mind and heart
Devoted wife and consistently passionate marriage
Articulate in my expression
Able to turn my experiences and stories into powerful frameworks for personal development for anyone looking to go in a new direction
Spend 9 months in a city and 3 months in a beautiful picturesque location

Notes:

50

Step 5 - Experience the future

Take a moment to lay down, close your eyes and really zone in on your answer to your last exercise / activity. Focus on you in 10 years time. What do you see? Where are you? Close your eyes, really let yourself explore your imagination and curiosities at that age in the future. Consider where you find yourself, how you feel and what you see around you in your life. After some time, when it feels right, open your eyes and write down everything you have imagined.

This should become something that you begin to practise regularly. It will help create a continuous chain of reaction that is engineered to galvanise you towards your most hopeful way of being. At times when you are letting your mind process you may start to see different ideas and options. These suggestions are there just for you to gain a sense of whether they will make you internally feel like your most empowered or whether they are just options that need no action. Just because you can see ideas and options doesn't mean they will all be right for you or true for who you really are. That being said, there is also a very strong chance that your heart already knows what it wants.When we find a few moments to close our eyes, calm our breath and see what is there for us in our minds eyes we gain a glimpse of our potential destiny. Once you have a notion of what you think will be an experience you will enjoy, it's wise to set up a small and significant experience that is 'safe to fail' so that you can taste the fruits without having to farm the land.

Naturally everyone reading this will be in completely different places with regard to the way they resonate with this topic. With this in mind I want to remind you that this book is for those that are deliberately trying to consciously create a new reality in their life. This is for those that are willing to try hard and think smart so they can pave the way to a better life experience. That does not mean this is the perfect way of being or the only way of being or that it is in fact a complete way of being at all. This whole book is just a supplement to daily life. A layer to add on top of the recipe that is already working for you.

Those that will be most successful in changing their life will first create the vision of their most desired, deepest, best, most heartfelt existence in this life within the landscape of their minds eye and inside their hearts. I do literally mean their hearts as well. It's possible to focus your mind's eye on your body parts, to feel your fingers, your shoulder, ears, nose, and toes without physical touch. You can also experience sensations in your heart and other organs.

When you are changing your life you simply need to get good at setting that visionary landscape, knowing how the sensations will feel when you are at your fullest, and being able to ruthlessly replan, reflect, improve, act and go again. Every time you find yourself falling off your most hopeful path, pick yourself back up again! Seek that vision, and go again! It's time!

Being in a continuous improvement cycle consciously is totally game changing. You begin paying attention to small details and soon you become blown away by the simple things in life. This makes peace and contentment simple and maximises your productivity time.

"If to change is to improve then to be perfect must mean to change frequently and often" - me, 2022.

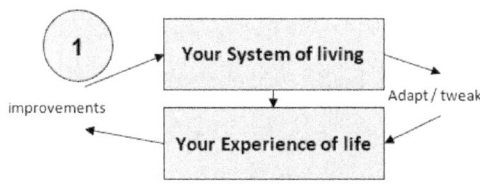

Sometimes we don't need to drastically rethink. Simply we need to new versions of the same decisions and use the new experiences to refresh our values and beliefs in their current form. Its a bit like dusting off the trophy cabinet of life. You reinforce healthy habits and consistent behaviours that are time proven by your own experience with a new found zest

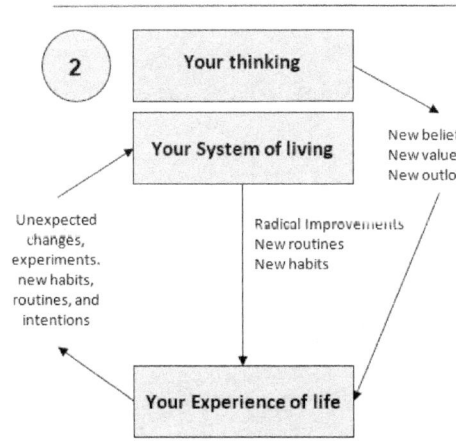

Other times you will find yourself challenging old ways of thinking. Maybe you become non-racist. Maybe you become religious. Maybe you become a fitness freak. Maybe you go vegan. Maybe you decide family is more important than your career. Or perhaps that spirituality is above wealth. Or maybe you chose the opposite... either way its for you to design and choose based on your most heartfelt desire. This is huge changes in your perception, it can build on your sense of identity, challenge your values and create brand new behaviour.

Huge changes in our underlying thinking and our outlook of life is changed forever. This is a very brave and bold moment. It is one that will make total sense to you and less to others around you (until they read this book!). That means you are being bold, you are being brave and you are breaking the mould - creating your own lane. Keep steadfast in your dreams, stay in touch with your subconscious by taking deliberate moments of reflection to consider your future in 10 years. Re-use the exercises in this book periodically and start to get into a cycle of deliberate experimentation.

It takes 3 weeks to develop neuroplasticity, which means you will start to feel more comfortable with the improvements you are experimenting with. After 6 weeks it becomes more normal to do the new consistent behaviour than to not do it. After 12 weeks you will notice the deeper impact of the new addition into your life. Given this, I now urge you to make three reminders in your phone calendar right now so you can reflect on your progress:

1) Make one right now in **exactly in 3 weeks** time from now

2) Make one right now in **exactly In 6 weeks** time from now

3) Make one right now in **exactly in 12 weeks** time from now

Now, hat are you going to focus on for the two segments below during that time?

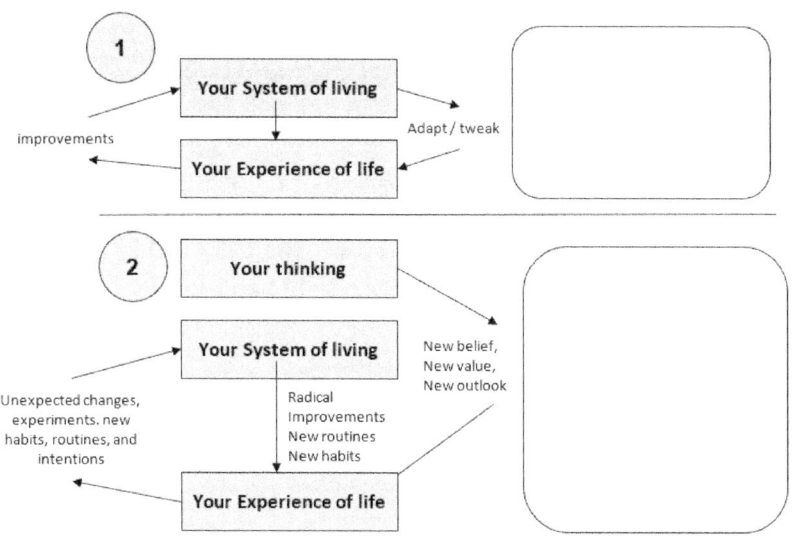

Notes:

Step 6 - Celebration

Congratulations on setting your intention for your highest, most meaningful, deepest experience of life!

Make a list of 10 things you are grateful for happening, occurring, existing, and yet to come in your life:

1.

2.

3.

4.

5.

6.

7.

8.

9.

10.

Reflect on what you have learnt about yourself and your ideas for the future by reading this book and completing every exercise. If you feel the book hasn't had the impact you thought it would, then I would urge you to make sure you did every exercise with your full conviction and a positive intent. Now that you have your vision in your landscape, all you can do is navigate your immediate environment in the best possible way. Whilst you take care of day to day business consistently and create 'your best life' where you are, then the ideas that you are ready will start to fly into your mind and grow in your soul. When these moments occur you need to truly go with the flow and bravely, boldly, allow life to suggest and guide your decision making. Continue to make 'safe to fail' experiments whenever you have the means so you either get you directly to your vision or evaluate safely whether it has the potential to be what you think it is.

Yours sincerely,
Rayyan Karim

Appendix

Whilst none of these books have been used directly, it is clear to me that these books had a significant impact on the way I think and the words I have written. Here they are for your further research, study and learnings:

- The Holy Quran

- Lao Tzu, The Tao Te Ching

- Sadghuru, Inner Engineering

- The life and teachings of Don Juan

- Adam Grant, Originals

- Alex Pentland, Social Physics

- James Allen, As a man thinketh

- Co-active Coaching, 4th Edition

- Simon Sinek, Start with why

- Tony Robbins, Wealth

- Thich Nhat Hanh, The miracle of Mindfulness

- Edward Deming, The Profound System of Knowledge

- Inayat Khan, The mysticism of sound and music

- Maurice Smith, This Is It

Your Space For Notes & Reflections

Your Space For Notes & Reflections

Printed in Great Britain
by Amazon

17036135R00037